Five mice like to ride bikes.
Five mice take a bike hike.
The mice ride and ride.

2

Five mice ride a mile.
The mice see piles of nuts.

Five mice dine on ripe nuts.
The mice get cups of lime ice.

3

4   Mike, the sad cat, hides in the pines.
Mike has no pals.

Five mice wave to Mike.
Do mice like cats?

5

6

Yes! Five mice like Mike.
The mice will be his pals.

But Mike has no bike.
Five mice yell, "Mike can jog!"

7

8

Five mice ride bikes.
Mike jogs.
The mice and Mike have a fine time!